100 Gospel Songs and Hymns for Trumpet and Guitar

With Suggested Chordal Accompaniment

By William Bay

WILLIAM
BAY MUSIC

Distributed by Mel Bay Publications, Inc.

WWW.MELBAY.COM

Index of Hymns

Title	Page

Title	Page

Preface

This is a collection of 100 favorite Gospel songs and hymns. Included are rousing camp meeting songs, sentimental expressions of a deep-rooted faith, and Gospel oriented hymns with a strong old-time music flavor. In preparing this collection I felt the sincere and solid faith of America's "revivalist era", staunchly embedded in the rural and Southern regions of America, but also in the dedicated inner city missions founded in sprawling urban centers.

These solos will bring joy, exuberance, nostalgia and a renewed sense of commitment to any worship celebration. They serve as a vehicle for and witness to the Christian faith.

Capo chords are included for the guitarist where appropriate. Slur and tempo markings are suggestions and are subject to the preference of the performer.

Additional books in this series are *100 Hymns for Trumpet and Guitar* and *100 Christmas Carols and Hymns for Trumpet and Guitar*.

William Bay

A Glorious Church

Guitar Capo 3rd Fret and Play the Chords in Parentheses

Fingerstyle or Strum Guitar Acc.

Ralph E. Hudson

arr. by William Bay

All the Way My Savior Leads Me

Guitar Capo 3rd Fret and Play the Chords in Parentheses

Fingerstyle or Strum Guitar Acc.

Robert Lowry
arr. by William Bay

Lyrically ♩ = 120

Amazing Grace

Fingerstyle or Strum Guitar Acc.

John Newton

arr. by William Bay

Swing Feeling ♩ = 92

America

Fingerstyle or Strum Guitar Acc.

Samuel A. Ward
arr. by William Bay

Are You Washed in the Blood?

Strum Guitar Acc.

Lively Tempo ♩ = 132

E. A. Hoffman

arr. by William Bay

Angel Band

Guitar Capo 3rd Fret and Play the Chords in Parentheses

Strum Guitar Acc.

William Bradbury
arr. by William Bay

(D) (A) (E) (A) (E) (A) (E)
F C G C G C G
64
(A) (E) (A) (E) (A) (D) (A)
C G C G C F C
72
(A) (F#m) (E) (A) (D) (A)
C Am G C F C
80
(A) (D) (E) (A)
C F G C
Guitar Tacit
88
rit.
(A) (E) (D) (A)
C G F C
96

As I Went Down to Pray

Strum Guitar Acc.

Joyfully ♩ = 100

American Spiritual
arr. by William Bay

At the Cross

Fingerstyle or Strum Guitar Acc.

Ralph E. Hudson
arr. by William Bay

Boldy ♩ = 112

13

Balm in Gilead

Spiritual

arr. by William Bay

Fingerstyle Guitar Acc.

Lyrically ♩ = 82

Blessed Assurance

Phoebe P. Knapp

arr. by William Bay

Strum or Fingerstyle Guitar Acc.

Lyrically ♩. = 74

Blessed Be the Name

Fingerstyle or Strum Guitar Acc.

Ralph E. Hudson
arr. by William Bay

Reverently ♩ = 90

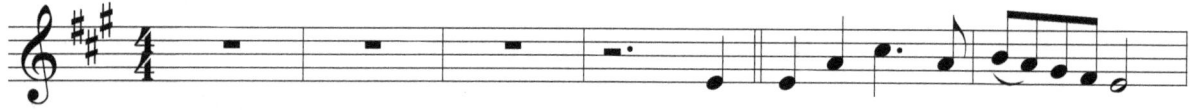

Blessed Quietness

W.S. Marshall
arr. by William Bay

Strum or Fingerstyle Guitar Acc.

Close to Thee

Fingerstyle Guitar Acc.

Silas J. Vail

arr. by William Bay

Relaxed Swing Feeling ♩ = 88

Death Has No Terrors

Guitar Capo 3rd Fret and Play the Chords in Parentheses

Strum Guitar Acc.

C.P. Jones

Boldly ♩ = 130

arr. by William Bay

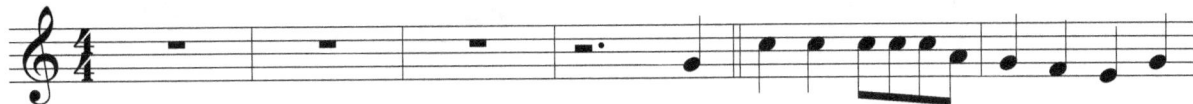

Down at the Cross

Strum or Fingerstyle Guitar Acc.

John H. Stockton

arr. by William Bay

Joyfully ♩ = 124

Draw Me Nearer

Guitar Capo 3rd Fret and Play the Chords in Parentheses

Strum Guitar Acc.

William H. Doane
arr. by William Bay

Moderately ♩ = 120

Drifting Too Far from the Shore

Guitar Capo 3rd Fret and Play the Chords in Parentheses

Fingerstyle Guitar Acc.

Charles E. Moody

arr. by William Bay

Every Bridge is Burned Behind Me

Strum Guitar Acc.

Lively ♩ = 134

George L. Hugg
arr. by William Bay

Every Day and Every Hour

Fingerstyle or Strum Guitar Acc.

William H. Doane

arr. by William Bay

Follow On

Guitar Capo 3rd Fret and Play the Chords in Parentheses

Strum Guitar Acc.

Robert Lowry

arr. by William Bay

Lively Tempo ♩ = 120

25

Every Time I Feel the Spirit

Guitar Capo the 3rd Fret and Play the Chords in Parentheses

Strum Guitar Acc.

Spiritual

arr. by William Bay

Joyfully ♩ = 142

(D) (G) (D) (A7) (D) (D) (A)
F B♭ F C7 F F C
33
(G) (D) (G) (D7)
(D) (A) (D) (A7)
F C F C7
B♭ F B♭ F7
37
1.
2.
E
(G) (G#dim) (D) (G) (D) (A7) (D) (G) (D7)
B♭ B dim7 F B♭ F C7 F B♭ F7
(G) (G#dim) (D) (G) (D) (A7) (D) (D7)
B♭ B dim F B♭ F C7 F F7
45
(G) (G#dim) (D) (G) (D) (A) (D) (Gdim)
B♭ B dim F B♭ F C F D♭dim
49
(G) (A7) (D)
B♭ C7 F
53

Glory to God, Hallelujah!

Guitar Capo 3rd Fret and Play the Chords in Parentheses

Strum Guitar Acc.

William J. Kirkpatrick
arr. by William Bay

Hallelujah, We Shall Rise

Strum Guitar Acc.

Joyfully ♩ = 126

J. E. Thomas
arr. by William Bay

Grace Greater Than Our Sin

Fingerstyle or Strum Guitar Acc.

Daniel B. Towner

arr. by William Bay

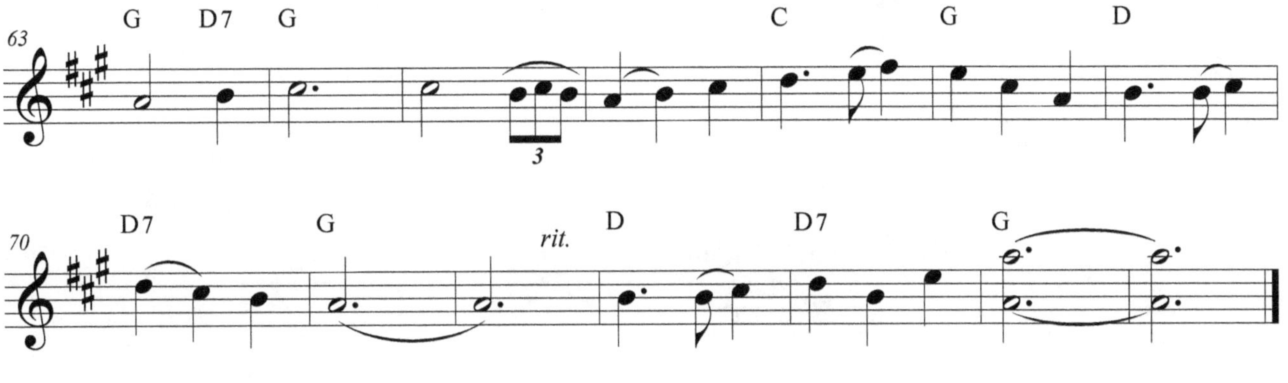
63
G D7 G
C G D
3
70
D7 G
rit.
D D7 G

Have Thine Own Way, Lord

Fingerstyle Guitar Acc.

George C. Stebbins

arr. by William Bay

Higher Ground

Fingerstyle Guitar Acc.

Charles H. Gabriel
arr. by William Bay

Lyrically ♩ = 88

Hold to God's Unchanging Hand

Fingerstyle or Strum Guitar Acc.

F. L. Eiland
arr. by William Bay

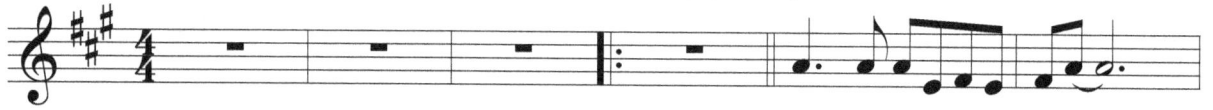

How Beautiful Heaven Must Be

Guitar Capo 3rd Fret and Play the Chords in Parentheses

Fingerstyle or Strum Guitar Acc.

A. P. Bland

arr. by William Bay

I Am Coming to the Cross

Guitar Capo 3rd Fret and Play the Chords in Parentheses

Fingerstyle or Strum Guitar Acc.

William G. Fischer

arr. by William Bay

I Am Resolved

I Feel Like Traveling On

Guitar Capo 3rd Fret and Play the Chords in Parentheses

Strum Guitar Acc.

William Hunter
arr. by William Bay

I Have Found the Way

I Love to Tell the Story

Fingerstyle Guitar Acc.

William G. Fischer

arr. by William Bay

I Need Thee Every Hour

I Will Praise Him

Guitar Capo 3rd Fret and Play the Chords in Parentheses

Fingerstyle Guitar Acc.

Margaret J. Harris
arr. by William Bay

I'll Live for Him

Guitar Capo 3rd Fret and Play the Chords in Parentheses

Fingerstyle Guitar Acc.

C.R. Dunbar

arr. by William Bay

In the Garden

In the Great Triumphant Morning

Strum Guitar Acc.

Joyfully ♩ = 140

R. E. Winsett
arr. by William Bay

Is Your All on the Altar?

Guitar Capo 3rd Fret and Play the Chords in Parentheses

Fingerstyle Guitar Acc.

Elisha A. Hoffman
arr. by William Bay

Flowing Tempo ♩ = 96

46

Just a Closer Walk with Thee

Fingerstyle or Strum Guitar Acc.

Anonynous

arr. by William Bay

Just As I Am

Guitar Capo 3rd Fret and Play the Chords in Parentheses

Fingerstyle Guitar Acc.

William Bradbury

arr. by William Bay

Keep on the Sunny Side of Life

Strum Guitar Acc.

J. Howard Entwisle
arr. by William Bay

Joyfully ♩ = 128

Just Over in the Gloryland

James W. Acuff and Emmett S. Dean

arr. by William Bay

Strum Guitar Acc.

Spirited ♩ = 130

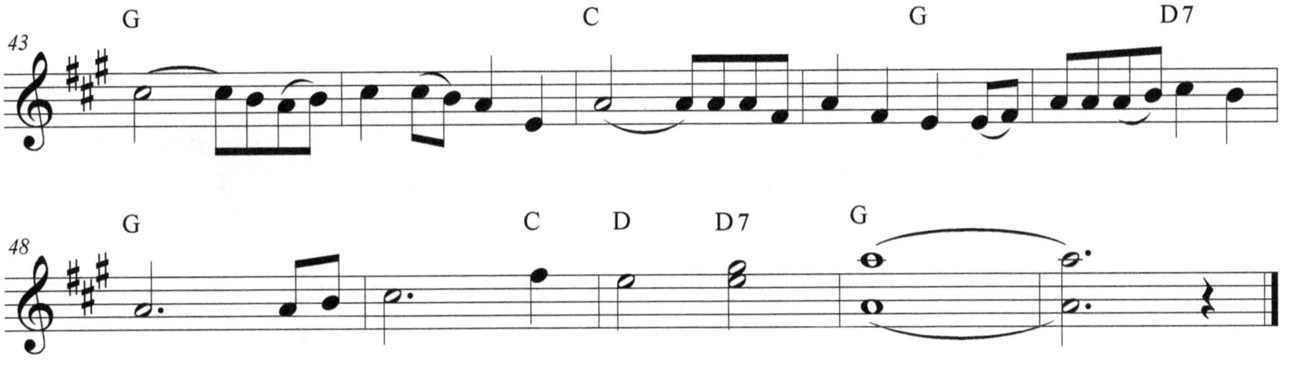
43
G
C
G
D7
48
G
C
D
D7
G

Leaning on the Everlasting Arms

Strum Guitar Acc.

Relaxed Swing Feeling ♩ = 128

Anthony J. Showalter
arr. by William Bay

Lord, I'm Coming Home

Fingerstyle or Strum Guitar Acc.

William J. Kirkpatrick

arr. by William Bay

Life is Like a Mountain Railroad

Strum Guitar Acc.

Charles D. Tillman
arr. by William Bay

Lively Tempo ♩ = 120

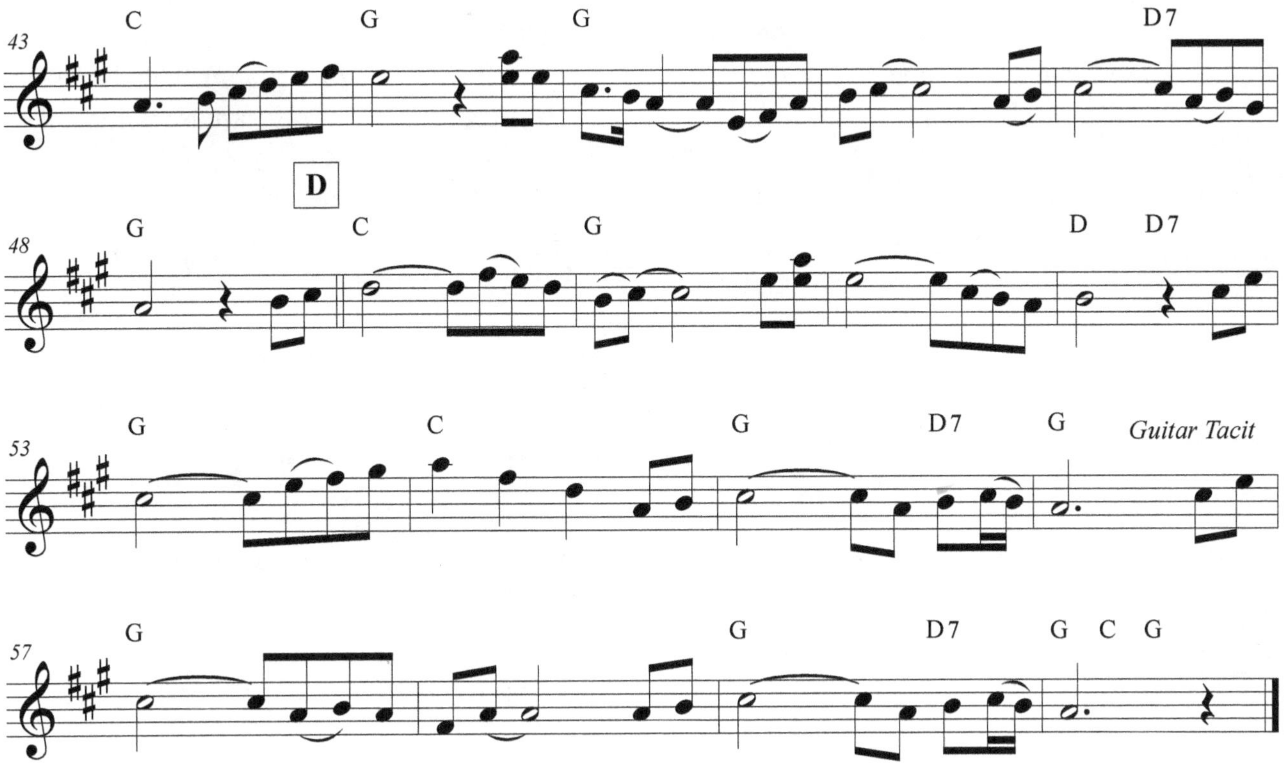
43
C
G
G
D7
D
48
G
C
G
D
D7
53
G
C
G
D7
G
Guitar Tacit
57
G
G
D7
G
C
G

More Love to Thee

Guitar Capo 3rd Fret and Play the Chords in Parentheses

Fingerstyle Guitar Acc.

William H. Doane

arr. by William Bay

Lyrically ♩ = 108

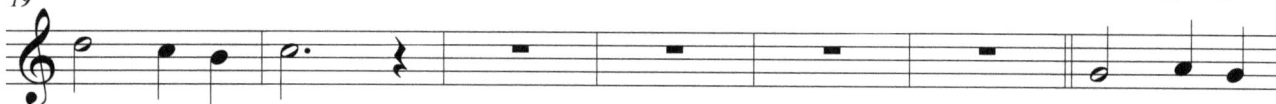

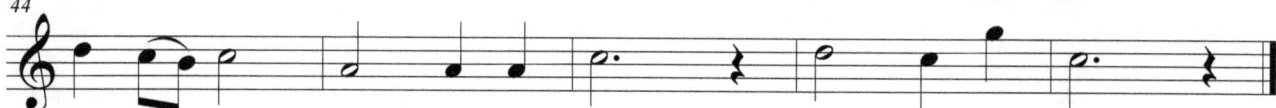

56

Must Jesus Bear the Cross Alone?

Guitar Capo the 3rd Fret and Play the Chords in Parentheses

Fingerstyle Guitar Acc.

George N. Allen
arr. by William Bay

Near the Cross

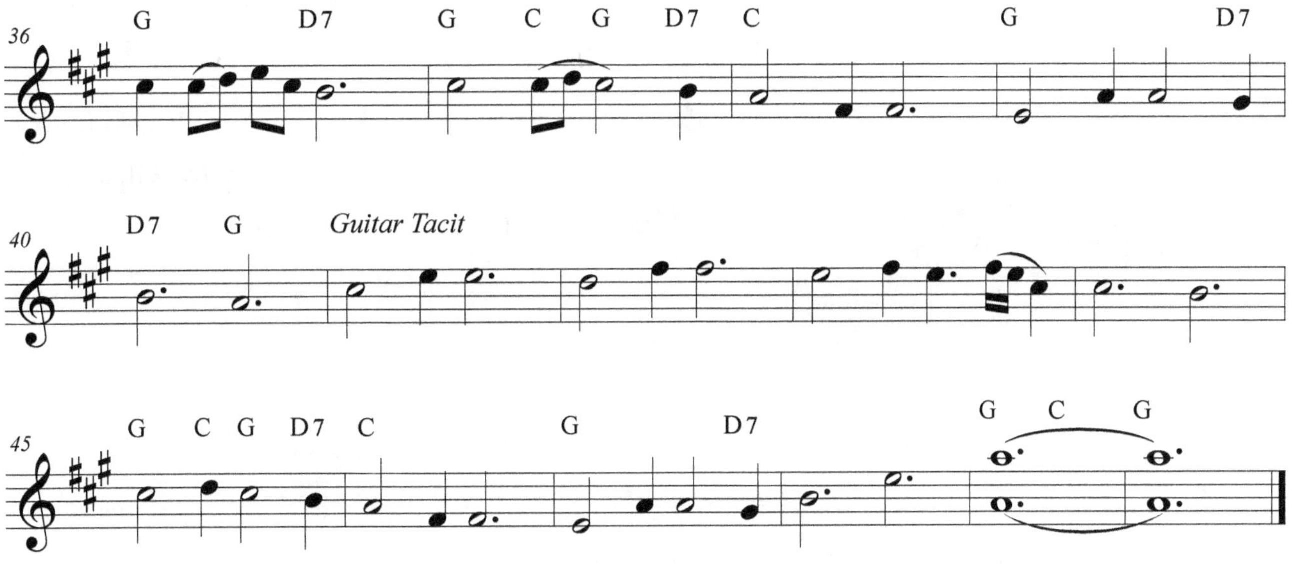
36
G D7 G C G D7 C G D7
40
D7 G
Guitar Tacit
45
G C G D7 C G D7 G C G

Nothing But the Blood

Strum Guitar Acc.

Robert Lowry
arr. by William Bay

O Store Gud
Often Sung as "How Great Thou Art"

Fingerstyle or Strum Guitar Acc.

Swedish Melody
arr. by William Bay

Majestically ♩ = 80

On Jordan's Stormy Banks

Guitar Capo 3rd Fret and Play the Chords in Parentheses

Only Trust Him

Fingerstyle or Strum Guitar Acc.

John H. Stockton
arr. by William Bay

Palms of Victory

Precious Memories

Fingerstyle Guitar Acc.

J. B. F. Wright

arr. by William Bay

Rock of Ages

Fingerstyle or Strum Guitar Acc.

Thomas Hastings
arr. by William Bay

Relaxed Swing Feeling ♩ = 80

Send the Light

Charles H. Gabriel
arr. by William Bay

Strum Guitar Acc.

Rhythmically ♩ = 118

Shall We Gather at the River

Guitar Capo 3rd Fret and Play the Chords in Parentheses

Robert Lowry
arr. by William Bay

Strum Guitar Acc.

Reverently ♩ = 84

Softly and Tenderly

Fingerstyle Guitar Acc.

Will L. Thompson
arr. by William Bay

Gently ♩. = 56

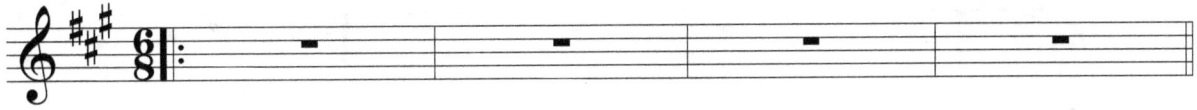

A

69

Something for Thee

Fingerstyle Guitar Acc.

Robert Lowry
arr. by William Bay

rit.

Standing on the Promises

Guitar Capo the 3rd Fret and Play the Chords in Parentheses

Strum Guitar Acc.

Russell Carter
arr. by William Bay

Rhythmically ♩ = 122

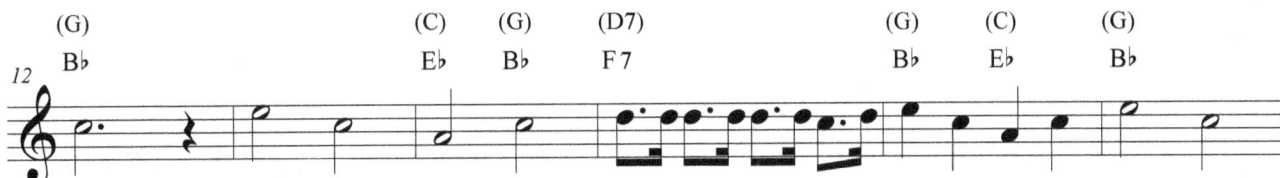
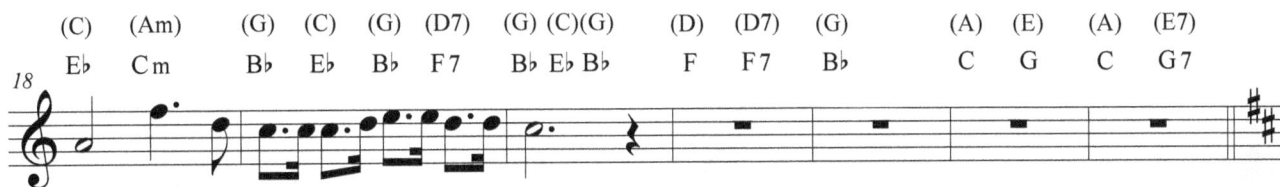

71

Sweet By and By

Guitar Capo the 4th Fret and Play the Chords in Parentheses

Strum Guitar Acc.

John R. Sweney
arr. by William Bay

Sweet Hour of Prayer

Guitar Capo the 3rd Fret and Play the Chords in Parentheses

Fingerstyle Guitar Acc.

William B. Bradbury
arr. by William Bay

73

Swing Low, Sweet Chariot

Fingerstyle or Strum Guitar Acc.

Spiritual
arr. by William Bay

Easy Swing Feeling ♩ = 86

Take the Name of Jesus with You

Fingerstyle or Strum Guitar Acc.

William H. Doane
arr. by William Bay

Relaxed Swing Feeling ♩ = 98

Take Time to Be Holy

Fingerstyle Guitar Acc.

George C. Stebbins
arr. by William Bay

The Church in the Wildwood

Guitar Capo the 3rd Fret and Play the Chords in Parentheses

Strum Guitar Acc.

William S. Pitts

arr. by William Bay

Rhythmically ♩ = 124

The Fire is Burning

Strum Guitar Acc.

George L. Hugg

arr. by William Bay

Lively Tempo ♩ = 128

The Gloryland Way

J. S. Torbett
arr. by William Bay

79

The Hallelujah Side

Strum Guitar Acc.

J. Howard Entwisle

arr. by William Bay

The Haven of Rest

Fingerstyle Guitar Acc.

George D. Moore
arr. by William Bay

Peacefully ♩ = 124

The Lily of the Valley

Guitar Capo 3rd Fret and Play the Chords in Parentheses

Strum Guitar Acc.

William S. Hays
arr. by William Bay

The Old Rugged Cross

Guitar Capo 3rd Fret and Play the Chords in Parentheses

Fingerstyle Guitar Acc.

George Bennard

arr. by William Bay

The Unclouded Day

84

50
G G7 C G G C G
56
D7 G G C G D7 G C
63
G G D D7 G
68
G C G D7 G C
73
G D7 G G C G
78
G D7 G C G C D
83
C D7 G D7 C G

The Valley of Blessing

William G. Fischer

arr. by William Bay

Fingerstyle or Strum Guitar Acc.

Relaxed Swing Feeling ♩ = 116

There is a Fountain

American Folk Melody
arr. by William Bay

Strum Guitar Acc.

Lively Tempo ♩ = 128

There is Glory in My Soul

Guitar Capo 3rd Fret and Play the Chords in Parentheses

Strum Guitar Acc.

Traditional

arr. by William Bay

Joyfully ♩ = 128

There is Joy Among the Angels

Strum Guitar Acc.

C. C. Case

arr. by William Bay

There is Power in the Blood

Guitar Capo 3rd Fret and Play the Chords in Parentheses

Strum Guitar Acc.

Traditional
arr. by William Bay

There's a Great Day Coming

Will L. Thompson
arr. by William Bay

There's a River of Life/Spring Up O Well

Strum Guitar Acc.

Joyfully ♩ = 124

L. Casebolt
arr. by William Bay

92

'Tis Burning in My Soul

Strum Guitar Acc.

William J. Kirkpatrick
arr. by William Bay

'Tis So Sweet to Trust in Jesus

To God Be the Glory

Triumph By and By

Strum Guitar Acc.

Joyfully ♩ = 120

H. R. Palmer
arr. by William Bay

Turn Your Eyes Upon Jesus

Guitar Capo 3rd Fret and Play the Chords in Parentheses

Fingerstyle Guitar Acc.

H.H. Lemmel
arr. by William Bay

97

We Shall Meet Someday

Guitar Capo 3rd Fret and Play the Chords in Parentheses

Strum Guitar Acc.

Tillit S. Teddlie

arr. by William Bay

Joyfully ♩ = 124

We'll Understand it Better By and By

Fingerstyle or Strum Guitar Acc.

Charles A. Tindley
arr. by William Bay

Swing Feeling ♩ = 116

We're Marching to Zion

What a Friend We Have in Jesus

Guitar Capo 3rd Fret and Play the Chords in Parentheses

Fingerstyle Guitar Acc.

Charles C. Converse

arr. by William Bay

What Must it Be to Be There

Strum Guitar Acc.

Joyfully ♩ = 124

George C. Stebbins
arr. by William Bay

When I Can Read My Title Clear

Strum Guitar Acc.

Robert Lowry
arr.by William Bay

When the Roll is Called Up Yonder

Where He Leads Me I Will Follow

J.S. Norris
arr. by William Bay

Fingerstyle Guitar Acc.

Lyrically ♩ = 82

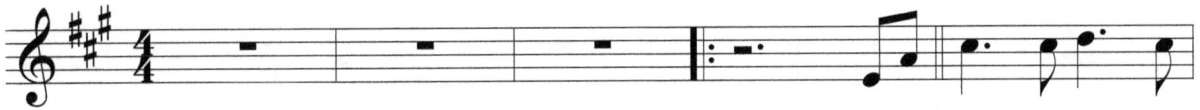

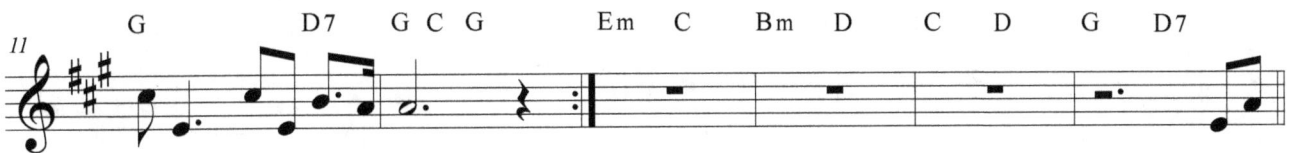

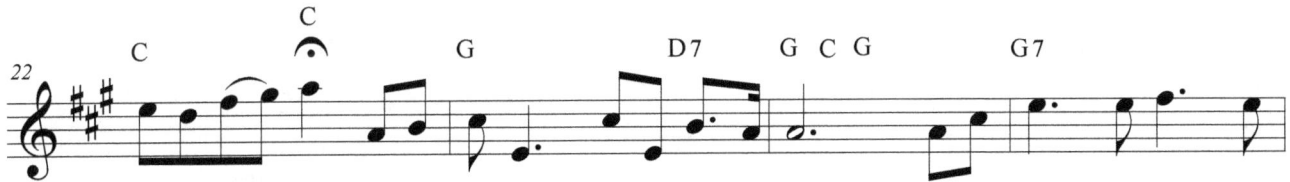

Where the Soul Never Dies

Strum Guitar Acc.

Lively 𝅗𝅥 = 116

Wm. M. Golden
arr. by William Bay

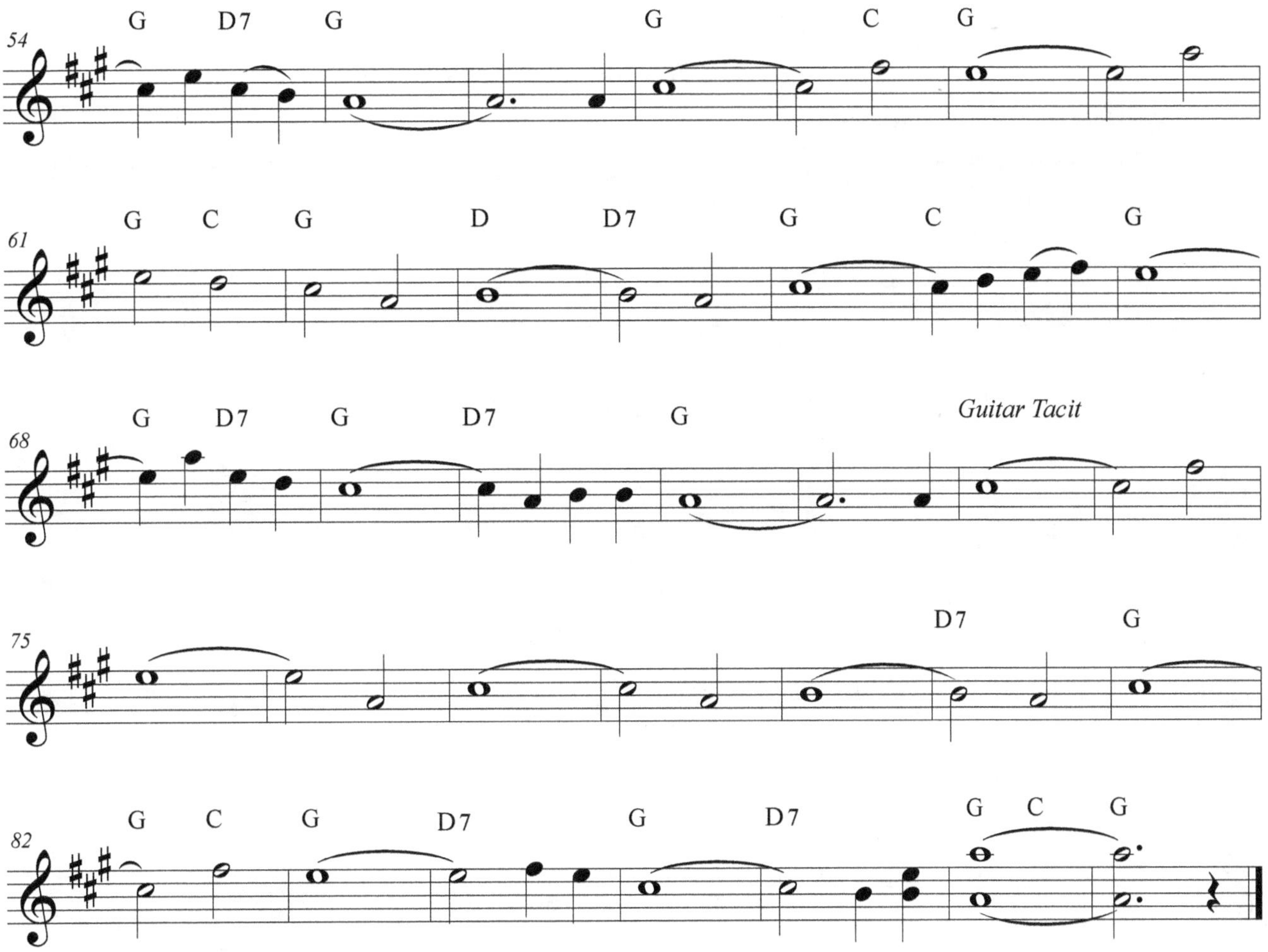
54
G D7 G G C G
61
G C G D D7 G C G
68
G D7 G D7 G
Guitar Tacit
75
D7 G
82
G C G D7 G D7 G C G

Where We'll Never Grow Old

Guitar Capo 3rd Fret and Play the Chords in Parentheses

Fingerstyle or Strum Guitar Acc.

James C. Moore

arr. by William Bay

Lyrically ♩ = 106

Whiter Than Snow

Fingerstyle or Strum Guitar Acc.

William G. Fischer
arr. by William Bay

Will the Circle Be Unbroken?

Charles H. Gabriel
arr. by William Bay

Wonderful Peace

Fingerstyle or Strum Guitar Acc.

W. G. Cooper
arr. by William Bay

Flowing Tempo ♩. = 72

Wonderful Words of Life

Fingerstyle Guitar Acc.

Philip P. Bliss
arr. by William Bay

Lyrically ♩. = 74

www.ingramcontent.com/pod-product-compliance
Lightning Source LLC
Chambersburg PA
CBHW081428090426
42740CB00017B/3227